Cars

by Dee Ready

Content Consultant:
Jon Hart
Marketing and Communications
Blackhawk Automotive Museum

Bridgestone Books

an imprint of Capstone Press

Bridgestone Books are published by Capstone Press
818 North Willow Street, Mankato, Minnesota 56001
http://www.capstone-press.com

Library of Congress Cataloging-in-Publication Data
Ready, Dee.
    Cars/by Dee Ready.
    p. cm.
    Includes bibliographical references and index.
    Summary: Briefly describes different types of cars, including sedans, station wagons, convertibles, race cars, and the Volkswagen "beetle."
    ISBN 1-56065-610-7
    1. Automobiles--Juvenile literature. [1. Automobiles.] I. Title.
TL147.R37   1998
629.222--dc21

97-12198
CIP
AC

Photo credits
Blackhawk Automotive Museum, 12
Betty Crowell, 8
Dodge, cover, 16
Ford Motor Company, 6
International Speedway Corp., 18
International Stock/Peter Lagone, 10
Chuck Place, 4
Shari Prange, 20
Unicorn Stock/Ed Harp, 14

Table of Contents

Cars

Cars are used to carry people and things. There are many different kinds of cars. Almost all cars have engines. An engine is a machine that moves a car. Most engines run on gas.

Sedans

A sedan is a car that carries four or more people. It has a front seat and a back seat. It can have two or four doors. It also has a trunk in back. A trunk is a space where things are stored.

Station Wagons

A station wagon is bigger than a sedan. Six or more people can ride in a station wagon. It has one or two back seats. The back seats can be folded down. This makes more space for carrying things.

Minivans

A minivan is bigger than a station wagon. It has more room to carry people and things. A minivan has a sliding door on the side. Sometimes it has two doors. Its doors make it easier to get in and out.

Convertibles

A convertible is a car with a special roof. The roof can be taken off or folded back. A convertible lets people enjoy nice weather.

Beetles

The Beetle is a small car first made in Germany. Sometimes it is called a Bug. It is not like most cars. It has a rounded body. Its engine is in back. Its trunk is in front.

Sports Cars

A sports car is made to go fast. It is a small car with a fast engine. A sports car has two bucket seats in the front. A bucket seat can hold only one person at a time.

Race Cars

A race car is made to win races. It usually carries only one person. A race car has a fast engine. It has wide wheels to help it stay on the track.

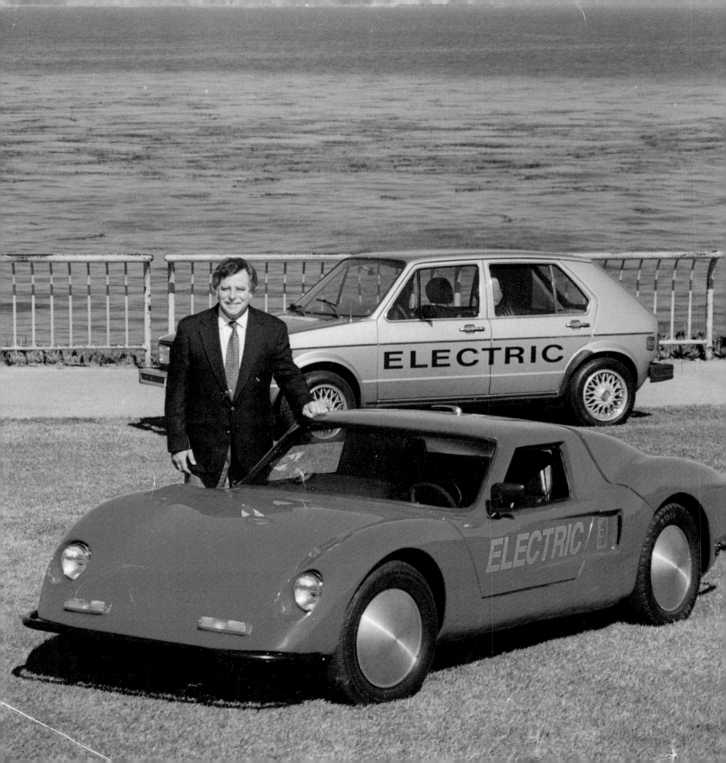

Electric Cars

An electric car runs on a battery instead of gas. A battery stores power. An electric car can run only one to two hours. Then the battery must be powered again. Electric cars keep the air cleaner than cars powered by gas.

Hands On: Streamlined Cars

Cars are becoming more streamlined. Streamlined means made to move more quickly through the air. Rounded cars move more quickly than boxy cars. Try this test to see how streamlining works.

What You Need:

A toy car   An index card
A penny   Tape
A bathtub with water

What You Do:

1. Fill your bathtub with water. The water is like the air cars move through.
2. Let your toy car roll down the side of the bathtub. Use the penny to mark where the car stops.
3. Stand the index card up on its short edge. Place it at the front of the car. Tape the bottom of the card to the car.
4. Fold the card over the car. Make the fold look like a box. Tape the end to the top of the car.
5. Roll the car down the side of the bathtub again. It will not travel as far as the first car.

The boxy car is not streamlined. This slows it down. A streamlined car goes faster.

Words to Know

battery (BAT-uh-ree)—an object that stores power

bucket seat (BUH-kit SEET)—a deep seat made to hold only one person

engine (EN-juhn)—a machine that moves things like cars

trunk (TRUHNGK)—a space where things are stored

Read More

Bendick, Jeanne. *The First Book of Automobiles*. New York: Franklin Watts, 1971.

Cooper, Jason. *Automobiles*. Vero Beach, Fla.: Rourke, 1991.

Rockwell, Anne. *Cars.* New York: Dutton Children's Books, 1984.

Royston, Angela. *Cars.* Eye Openers. New York: Aladdin Books, 1991.

Internet Sites

Blackhawk Automotive Museum
http://www.blackhawkauto.org
The Otto Club
http://www.ottoclub.org

Index